JAVA

PROGRAMMING 2022

HOW TO BE THE BEST DEVELOPER:
TOP SECRETS OF JAVA LANGUAGE

Java Programming 2022:

How To Be The Best Developer: Top Secrets Of Java Language

* Java Programming

There are many programming dialects available and each one in all them is suitable for every other application or utility. There are people who've learnt multiple programming dialects and who make use of those in mild of the reality that this is the aspect that they realize, bust the giant majority of the activities programming builders will make use of the programming language this is wished via way of means of the utility they're making. Java is pretty probable the maximum habitually applied programming language and writing on this language is a few manner or every other now no longer similar to the same old Pascal or any C/C++ shape but that does not suggest that studying the java code is extra earnestly than studying Pascal or C++. These days there are numerous programs written in Java and its wording it'd appear like a chunk more difficult withinside the first area but every person can write on this programming language, this is in reality.

When investigating every other programming language, the giant majority may need to realize whether or not it isn't always tough to study and paintings in. In the occasion which you comparison it with C or C++, you may locate that undoubtedly, using it thoroughly can be all of the extra immediately forward. This is due to the manner that Java has some distance much less amazements contrasted with C forms. C and C++ make use of a ton of traits so studying and dominating all of them may be an amazing challenge (for instance, impermanent elements live close by lengthy get-togethers paintings that made them has ended). Being all of the extra immediately forward, Java is incredibly easier to study and to paintings with. Java wipes out unequivocal pointer dereferences and reminiscence distribution/recovery, for instance, of the maximum muddled wellsprings of insects for C and C++ software program engineers. Out of attain addendums aren't tough to song down, as Java can do upload cluster limits checking. Others may contend that it seems to be easier to paintings with considering the fact that there aren't many times of pretty convoluted undertakings accomplished using it, but the average stated concept is that it's miles via way of means of one manner or every other easier to dominate than C or C++.

Learning Java writing laptop applications is distinctly easy, specially if you realize approximately different, extra essential, programming dialects and you recognize in reality what you want to make using it and it has a development of blessings contrasted with C and C++. Above all else, code written on this programming language is compact. Code written in C and C++ is not and this makes Java extra viable (for instance, in C and C++, each execution chooses the exactness and potential requirements for crucial statistics types.

At the factor while you want to transport beginning with one framework then onto the next, that is a reason of troubles due to the fact adjustments in numeric exactness can have an impact on estimations). Then again, Java characterizes the scale of crucial sorts for all executions (for instance, an "int" on one framework is a comparable length and it addresses comparable scope of characteristics as on every and each different given framework).

The times of tasks that make use of skimming factor math calls for a completely unique consideration: a application that utilizations coasting factor computations can supply numerous solutions on numerous frameworks (for this situation, the extent of difference increments with the amount of estimations a selected really well worth is going through). However, that is a aspect express to all skimming factor code, now no longer simply Java code which is also extra flexible then C or C++ in its object code. It arranges to an editorial code for a hypothetical machine - on the quit of the day, the translator imitates that machine. This approach the manner that code accrued on one PC will run on different PC machines that has a Java translator, but extra concerning this count you may find out at the same time as studying Java programming.

* Best Way To Learn Java Programming

A commercial enterprise may be basically depicted as Java programming has been withinside the the front line withinside the realm of Information Technology development. This may be higher visible inner an organisation's IT development. Frequently almost about company development Java is being applied. One real version in which this programming language is being applied is on an organisation express device as an example plane booking. Have you at any factor concept how plane corporations make it easier to ee-e book a journey enormously speedy via way of means of basically signing into the framework? Because of Java that is made viable.

Few out of each abnormal software program engineer is distinct and has taken in each one of the ropes approximately Java. Some may realize the nuts and bolts but a tad of the excessive stage ones. This is the area in which a software program engineer who desires to dominate on this subject have to do the whole thing to study Java programming. How may want to this be viable while you had the possibility to shuffle out of your 8-hour paintings 5 days every week and were given some duties too? Beneficial aspect that the Internet is loaded up with property which you may use to your ability advantage. You have to without a doubt to move get an character who is aware of Java, can display you one-on-one at some point of your more energy, and has sufficient property to impart to you approximately this thoughts boggling programming language.

Indeed, the maximum best method to study Java writing laptop applications is as a way to have a manual or instruct who've the tolerance to provide you a survey approximately the nuts and bolts and help you with studying the improvement stuff. Be extraordinarily organized to pay out coins incredibly a extra quantity of what you anticipate specially assuming you want to advantage from the nice person. Aside from the statistics which you may accumulate from it, you may likewise refresh your self with the maximum current variations.

To date there are an combination of seven styles of Java for the reason that major arrival of JDK 1.1 manner lower back in February 19, 1997. The present day shape is Java SE7 which become added in July 28, 2011. Update nine for this Java 7 has been added as of past due on October 16, 2012.

As have to be obvious, at the off danger which you have found out Java manner lower back in 1997 and you haven't refreshed your self with the maximum current variations similarly to everything of the updates you may be abandoned. Thusly, it's miles honestly an unquestionable requirement to study Java programming and replace your variety of abilities.

Not the essential however alternatively a extra quantity of upgrading your learning and cappotential simultaneously.

* Why Learn Java?

Java is a slicing aspect item located programming language

Item organized writing laptop applications is a fashion of plan that endeavors to show gadgets in fact using devices of PC code referred to as classes. This programming fashion has been exhibited to strengthen code this is each strong and adaptable. As properly as being item located java guide different present day programming strategies, as an example, multithreading, mistake manipulate using exemptions, and traditional programming.

Java has a spotless and dependable language shape

The Java language become deliberate with none preparation. Its draftsmen did not should pressure over similarity with beyond dialects as had the choice to provide Java an excellent and consistent punctuation. This makes the language further easy to study and satisfactory to application in. It moreover allows recorded as a difficult replica reliable programs.

Java is extensively applied

Java is applied in commercial enterprise, instruction, designing and technical studies, definitely its applied pretty properly anyplace PCs are applied. Assuming you are an professional developer or programmer, or considering turning into one, being succesful in Java will genuinely do your career and financial institution stability no damage.

Java comes general

Java comes general with a big green Application Programmers Interface

(API). This allows the software program engineer to assume the factors of hobby of an challenge with out composing extra vast code or to monkey approximately with outsider libraries.

Java become meant to be flexible

Most Java tasks will run with nearly no alteration on a huge variety of operating frameworks in addition to system stages.

Java is an organisation pushed language Java become meant to feature admirably in prepared situations, its API and safety version make community programming covered and strong.

Java is secure

Java is secure, it allows code from the internet to be run in a secluded weather, protective the host framework from infections and so forth Also the Java API offers schedules for coping with automated declarations and different cryptographic strategies.

Java is an exemplary language

Java can sensibly be referred to as an exemplary language. Later appearances, like C#, owe a amazing deal to Java. This sample will probably proceed. This implies time spent studying Java will income you even get-togethers will become vintage due to the fact its substitutions will in all likelihood imitate a whole lot of its language shape and programming fashion.

Synopsis

The important challenge is, at the off danger which you study Java you may be cheerful, wealthy and properly acknowledged, little youngsters will want to be you, absolute outsiders will want to have your children, your severa memoirs might be blockbusters for pretty a protracted time, your Nobel prizes have to account to your Fields awards at the shelf piece of your masterful domestic and honest younger manufacturers from the BBC will want to make narratives approximately you and your numerous accomplishments.

* How To Become A Java Developer?

Know Java's Strengths

Java is one in all many programming dialects withinside the IT commercial enterprise. You might also additionally even realize a pair of those dialects as of now, or might also additionally have acknowledged approximately them - ASP, C, PHP are most effective a pair fashions. Anyway, with those fashions, for what cause wouldn't it not be an awesome concept as a way to go along with Java?

I'm now no longer right here to mention that Java is the excellent maximum enormously horrible language. What I'd choose to make connection with is that Java has its area, and also you want to realize it is characteristics. Java is a first rate language for full-size frameworks, and ones that want the exhibition and flexibility that Java offers. It is maximum probable now no longer the nice language choice for extra modest obligations or extra modest webweb sites - it is viable but it is now no longer in which Java's characteristics lie.

Download The Necessary Tools

To begin studying Java you will should down load the apparatuses and programming to create with. You'll require matters - the Java Development Kit (JDK) and an development weather (in any other case referred to as an IDE, which represents Integrated Development Environment). Some IDEs which are very well-known are NetBeans and Eclipse.

These are each available from the Java site. Whenever you have downloaded and added them, it is a really perfect possibility to start studying the language.

Become acquainted with The Java Language

To develop into a Java fashion dressmaker you want to discern out a way to application in Java. In the occasion which you genuinely realize a number of it, this is great - it's going to make this component easier. If now no longer, you may discern out a way to application in Java from some sources:

- Web-primarily based totally educational physical activities. Numerous webweb sites provide educational physical activities at the nice manner to create in Java, from beginner thoughts to slicing aspect subjects. Do a Google seek to song down a few that paintings for you.

- Textbooks - Buying a direction ee-e book is a first rate approach to get acquainted with the language, because it likewise carries beginner and stepped forward thoughts. Large numbers of them have sports and fashions that are beneficial.

- Courses at university or school. A amazing deal of faculties or schools provide brief guides and a few may comprise Java development. This enjoys the advantage of being in a meeting weather and having an instructor, in place of self-gaining from a ee-e book or site.

Start Your Own Java Project

Whenever you've got got the necessities dealt with, you may start your very own challenge to help with propelling your Java abilities. This may be something you like. The factor is to rehearse and foster your Java abilities, so you are extra gifted approximately the Java development language and the way to make use of the IDE. You'll get beneficial revel in on troubleshooting, fostering your very own code, and adhering to nice practices. These matters need to had been won out of your educational exercising or different studying techniques, but setting them into usage is a first rate approach to enhance those abilities.

Make The Next Stride

When you are sure approximately your Java development capacities, it is a really perfect possibility to make the subsequent stride - touchdown that Java development position. This is maximum probable the toughest piece of the interaction. Many corporations have one of a kind revel in prerequisites, that could comprise certificates, ranges and professional revel in.

In case you are without a doubt studying the language and don't have any professional revel in, you need to be looking for phase stage Java positions. These kind of positions may require a few kind of confirmation or displaying of your capacities. This is the area in which your facet challenge comes in - withinside the occasion which you've built programs or webweb sites using Java, it thoroughly can be applied for your resume to assist your odds.

Another amazing tip for the way to show right into a Java fashion dressmaker is to get guaranteed. An amazing affirmation first of all is the SCJA - Sun Certified Java Associate. This accreditation is right for understudies or phase stage Java software program engineers and might be an great gain to you while looking for a project as a Java fashion dressmaker. Examine every other new article at the maximum gifted approach to show right into a developer to study extra tips.

* Most Significant Advantages Of Java Language

Java has obtained big occurrence because it to begin with confirmed up. Its speedy growing and huge acknowledgment may be accompanied to its plan and programming highlights, specially in its assure that you may compose a application once, and run it anyplace. Java become picked because the programming language for community PCs (NC) and has been visible as a great the front quit for the undertaking statistics base. As expressed in Java language white paper via way of means of Sun Microsystems: "Java is a straightforward, item-organized, conveyed, deciphered, vigorous, secure, layout nonpartisan, compact, multi strung, and dynamic."

Java(TM) enjoys essential higher fingers over distinct dialects and situations that make it suitable for quite a lot any programming project.

The advantages of Java are as in keeping with the subsequent:

o Java isn't always tough to study.

Java become meant to be now no longer tough to make use of and is therefore easy to compose, assemble, troubleshoot, and study than different programming dialects.

o Java is item-organized. This allows you to make precise tasks and reusable code.

o Java is level free.

Perhaps the primary advantages of Java is its potential to transport efficiently beginning with one PC framework then onto the next. The potential to run comparable application on numerous frameworks is critical to World Wide Web programming, and Java prevails at this via way of means of being level independent at each the supply and twofold levels.

o Java is disseminated.

Java is meant to make disseminated registering easy with the structures management cappotential this is innately integrated into it. Composing community applications in Java resembles sending and getting statistics to and from a document.

o Java is secure.

Java thinks approximately safety as a function of its plan. The Java language, compiler, mediator, and runtime weather had been every developed in mild of safety.

o Java is hearty.

Hearty approach unwavering quality. Java places a ton of accentuation on early checking for ability blunders, as Java compilers can apprehend severa troubles that could first seem at some point of execution time in pretty a at the same time as.

o Java is multithreaded.

Multithreaded is the cappotential for a application to play out some assignments on the equal time inner a application. In Java, multithreaded programming has been perfectly integrated into it, at the same time as in distinct dialects, operating framework express strategies should be delivered to empower multithreading.

As a end result of Java's strength, usability, cross-level capacities and safety highlights, it has end up a language of choice for giving average Internet arrangements.

SARA JACKLINE

www.ingramcontent.com/pod-product-compliance
Lightning Source LLC
Chambersburg PA
CBHW080923160726
48000CB00009B/3107